Children of Native America Today

Yvonne Wakim Dennis & Arlene Hirschfelder
With a foreword by Buffy Sainte-Marie

SHAKTI for Children
Charlesbridge

Dennis—Husband, partner, chef, humorist, traveler, and dog-lover extraordinaire—my thanks for being all of these and more.
—A. H.

Roger—*Wado* for your vision, spirit, mind, ears, encouragement, and especially all your love.
—Y. W. D.

Children of Native America Today is a project of SHAKTI for Children, which is dedicated to teaching children to value diversity. SHAKTI for Children is a program of The Global Fund for Children: www.globalfundforchildren.org.

Population figures are taken from the United States Census 2000 unless otherwise noted.

Developed by SHAKTI for Children
The Global Fund for Children
1101 14th Street NW, Suite 910
Washington, D.C. 20005
(202) 331-9003
www.shakti.org

Published by Charlesbridge
85 Main Street
Watertown, MA 02472
(617) 926-0329
www.charlesbridge.com

Library of Congress Cataloging-in-Publication Data

Hirschfelder, Arlene B.
  Children of native America today / Arlene Hirschfelder and Yvonne Wakim Dennis
      p. cm.
Summary: Text and photographs introduce traditions, activities, and lifestyles of children from various North American tribes.
  ISBN 1-57091-499-0 (reinforced for library use)
  1. Indian children—North America—Juvenile literature. 2. Indians of North America—Social life and customs—Juvenile literature. [1. Indians of North America.] I. Dennis, Yvonne Wakim. II. Title.
  E98.C5 .H66 2003
  306'.08997073'083—dc21   2002002272

Printed in South Korea
(hc) 10 9 8 7 6 5 4 3 2 1

Color separations by Pacifica Communications, South Korea
Printed and bound by Pacifica Communications, South Korea

Contents

Buffy Sainte-Marie

FOUNDER, THE NIHEWAN FOUNDATION
The Nihewan Foundation is a non-profit corporation founded in 1969. Its programs include scholarships, teacher training, the Cradleboard Teaching Project, and the Youth Council on Race.

Foreword

Many children want to know about Native American people and cultures. Many teachers would like to help them learn. The need for enriching, accurate teaching materials in mainstream education about American Indians has never been greater—especially for teachers of younger children, since there are so many different Native cultures, and each one is so rich.

All children belong to at least one culture group. We can strengthen every child's personal identity and interest in their own and other cultures by providing great materials and engaging their curiosity. This book is a collection of brief profiles of Native American tribes and culture groups designed to give school-age children a snapshot of the wealth of information there is to learn.

During the five years that I spent on *Sesame Street*, I tried to convey in the Native American episodes one message above all: Indians Exist. We are alive and real. We have fun, friends, families, and a whole lot to contribute to the rest of the world through our reality. The Cradleboard Teaching Project, a program of the Nihewan Foundation, is one way to get this message across. Cradleboard helps children get to know one another through cross-cultural communication, using whatever means they have.

Native American children, like all children, are not only their cultures. Even kids from the most traditional Native backgrounds have much in common with all other children: they have families, they grow and change every day, they love and work and play.

Many Native American children, through their families and communities, experience a special cultural richness. These kids understand that they live in a special relationship between the earth and the sky; that they are related to all other creatures; that their cultures are unique and precious. They also know many hard truths: that their native languages are greatly endangered; that their ancestors experienced hatred and violence in their own country; that much of their greatness is unknown to most other people.

But Native children, like all children, should also know that there is tremendous good work to be done in which they can share. They have a future.

Buffy Sainte-Marie

Authors' Preface

Do you know what it means to stereotype? People stereotype others when they present a group of people in the same way all the time, usually negatively. American Indian people, for instance, are often depicted as mean, wearing feathers and beads and carrying bows and arrows. Books and movies rarely show them even living in the 21st century!

This is a book of few words and many pictures. You will begin to learn that Native children live in many different places, speak many different languages, and have many different cultures and customs. When we selected the groups to include in this book, we tried to show this diversity. We chose tribes from across the country, native peoples of Alaska and Hawaii, small and large nations, and confederations made up of several tribes. Native people living in cities are in this book, too. We picked some groups whose ancestors were forced to relocate from their homelands.

Yet the nations in this book are just a few of more than 500 Native cultures. As you will see, Native children can participate in their ancient customs and also ride bikes, play video games, and attend school like other American children. Their parents work like any other adults and they live in houses like other Americans.

Imagine if someone came to your house and made you move away or destroyed your home. Imagine if many of your relatives and friends died trying to save their homes and their way of life. That is what happened to Native people when Europeans first came here over 500 years ago. It is important to learn the truth about Native peoples, the original inhabitants of this land. Native cultures were here long before the United States was a country. Native peoples and communities still face many problems today and constantly fight court battles to maintain their rights and status as independent nations—their sovereignty.

If you are a Native child reading this book, we hope you find out something you didn't know about another Native nation. If you are a non-Native child, we hope that you will forget untrue and unkind things you may have learned about Native peoples. This book has a tiny bit of the vast information about Indian people. There is a lot more to learn.

Yvonne Wakim Dennis and Arlene Hirschfelder

It does not require many words to speak the truth.

Chief Joseph, Nee-Mee-Poo
(Nez Perce)

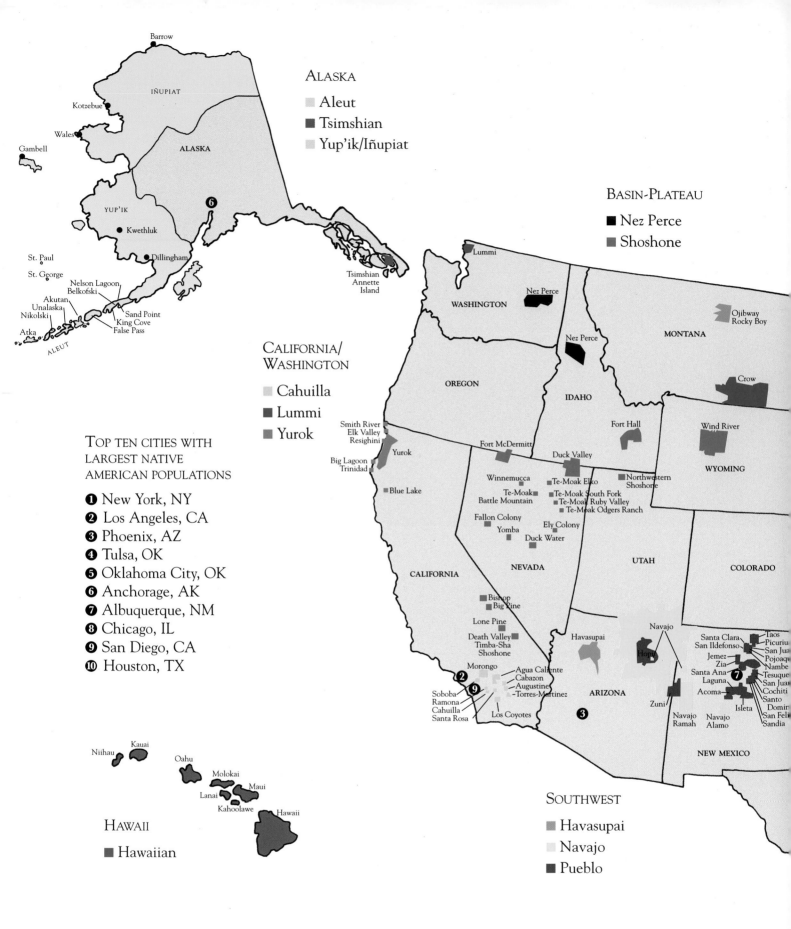

ALASKA
- Aleut
- Tsimshian
- Yup'ik/Iñupiat

Barrow

IÑUPIAT

Kotzebue

Wales

ALASKA

Gambell

YUP'IK

Kwethluk

St. Paul
St. George

Dillingham

Nelson Lagoon
Belkofski
Akutan
Unalaska
Nikolski
Atka

Sand Point
King Cove
False Pass

ALEUT

Tsimshian
Annette
Island

BASIN-PLATEAU
- Nez Perce
- Shoshone

CALIFORNIA/
WASHINGTON
- Cahuilla
- Lummi
- Yurok

TOP TEN CITIES WITH
LARGEST NATIVE
AMERICAN POPULATIONS

❶ New York, NY
❷ Los Angeles, CA
❸ Phoenix, AZ
❹ Tulsa, OK
❺ Oklahoma City, OK
❻ Anchorage, AK
❼ Albuquerque, NM
❽ Chicago, IL
❾ San Diego, CA
❿ Houston, TX

Lummi

WASHINGTON

Nez Perce

MONTANA

Ojibway
Rocky Boy

Nez Perce

OREGON

IDAHO

Crow

Fort Hall

Wind River

WYOMING

Smith River
Elk Valley
Resighini

Fort McDermitt

Duck Valley

Big Lagoon
Trinidad

Yurok

Winnemucca

Te-Moak Elko

Northwestern
Shoshone

Blue Lake

Te-Moak
Battle Mountain

Te-Moak South Fork
Te-Moak Ruby Valley
Te-Moak Odgers Ranch

Fallon Colony

Yomba

Ely Colony

Duck Water

NEVADA

UTAH

COLORADO

CALIFORNIA

Bishop
Big Pine

Lone Pine

Death Valley
Timba-Sha
Shoshone

Navajo

Santa Clara
San Ildefonso

Taos
Picuriu
San Jua

Havasupai

Jemez
Zia

Pojoaqu
Nambe

Hopi

Santa Ana

Tesuque

Morongo

Agua Caliente
Cabazon
Augustine
Torres-Martinez

❷
❾

Soboba
Ramona
Cahuilla
Santa Rosa

Los Coyotes

ARIZONA

❸

Zuni

Laguna

Acoma

San Jua
Cochiti
Santo
Domi
San Feli
Sandia

❼

Isleta

Navajo
Ramah

Navajo
Alamo

NEW MEXICO

Niihau

Kauai

Oahu

Molokai

Lanai

Maui

Kahoolawe

Hawaii

HAWAII
- Hawaiian

SOUTHWEST
- Havasupai
- Navajo
- Pueblo

6

Communities in *Children of Native America Today*

PLAINS
- Comanche
- Crow
- Lakota

CENTRAL
- Cherokee
- Meskwaki
- Ojibway

NORTHEAST
- Haudenosaunee
- Wabanaki
- Wampanoag

SOUTHEAST
- Choctaw
- Lumbee
- Powhatan
- Seminole

Turtle Mountain
NORTH DAKOTA
Standing Rock and Cheyenne River
Crow Creek and Lower Brulé
SOUTH DAKOTA
Pine Ridge and Rosebud
NEBRASKA
KANSAS
OKLAHOMA
Cherokee Nation of Oklahoma
Seminole Nation of Oklahoma
United Keetowah, Band of Cherokee
Comanche Tribe
Meskwaki (Sac and Fox)
Seneca Cayuga Tribe of Oklahoma
Choctaw Nation of Oklahoma
TEXAS

Red Lake
Bois Forte
Leech Lake
White Earth
Fond Du Lac
Mille Lacs
St. Croix
MINNESOTA
IOWA
Meskwaki
MISSOURI
Cherokee
ARKANSAS
LOUISIANA
Choctaw

Grand Portage
Ontonagon
Red Cliff
Bad River
Keweenaw
Bay Mills
Sault St. Marie
MICHIGAN
Lac Vieux Desert
Lac Courte Oreilles
Lac Du Flambeau
Sokaogon
Oneida
WISCONSIN
Burt Lake
Grand Traverse
Isabella/ Saginaw
MICHIGAN
ILLINOIS
INDIANA
OHIO
KENTUCKY
Cherokee
TENNESSEE
Cherokee
MISSISSIPPI
Mississippi Band of Choctaw Indians
Cherokee
ALABAMA
GEORGIA
Cherokee

Arrostock Band-Micmac
Houlton-Maliseet
Indian Township-Passamaquoddy
MAINE
Penobscot
Pleasant Point-Passamaquoddy
Abenaki
VERMONT
NEW HAMP-SHIRE
Mohawk Akwesasne/ St. Regis
Oneida
MASSACHUSETTS
Abenaki
Mashpee-Wampanoag
Aquinnah-Wampanoag
RHODE ISLAND
CONNECTICUT
Tuscarora
Seneca Tonawanda
Onondaga
Kanatsiohareke
Cayuga
NEW YORK
Seneca Cattaraugus
Seneca Oil Springs
Seneca Allegany
PENNSYLVANIA
NEW JERSEY
MARYLAND
DELAWARE
WEST VIRGINIA
VIRGINIA
Rappahannock
Powhatan
Mattaponi
Pamunkey
Chickahominy
Nansemond
Eastern Chickahominy
Cherokee
NORTH CAROLINA
Pembroke
Lumbee
Cherokee
SOUTH CAROLINA
FLORIDA
Fort Pierce
Tampa
Brighton
Big Cypress
Immokalee
Hollywood

7

Wabanaki (WAH-beh-NOCK-ee)

All dressed up in ribbon shirts for Recognition Day, Maliseet

Playing games at the University of Vermont Powwow, Vermont Abenaki

Go almost as far east as you can and you will be in Wabanaki territory. *Wabanaki* means "people of the dawn land." The Wabanaki Confederacy includes the Penobscot, Passamaquoddy, Micmac, and Maliseet people of Maine, and the Abenaki of Vermont and other New England states. The United States and Canadian borders separate the original Wabanaki lands of dense forests and rivers.

Blue is the color of the Passamaquoddy tribe's Northeastern Blueberry Company in Columbia Falls, Maine, during harvest time. It is the third largest blueberry farm in the world. You can get pretty blue picking blueberries! Besides the farm, the Passamaquoddy own radio stations, a cable program, and some small manufacturing plants.

Have you ever searched for a giant moose? The Passamaquoddy look for moose by airplane and on foot, to see how well the herd is doing. The Passamaquoddy communities of Pleasant Point and Indian Township are 50 miles apart. Although people usually drive from one community to the other, sometimes they go by canoe. You can learn a lot about the Passamaquoddy by visiting the Wapohnaki Museum in Sipayik, Maine.

The Penobscot reservation includes over 100 islands in the Penobscot River. Take a guided canoe trip to see moose and eagles, or visit the Penobscot museum to see famous birchbark art and baskets. In August everyone gets together for homecoming. The fun includes storytelling, talking circles, and a bike rodeo!

On Indian Island, Penobscot workers manufacture toys and audiocassettes. Micmacs make beautiful baskets available by mail order. Look for Maine potatoes in the grocery store—some are raised on the fertile Maliseet farms. The Abenaki in Franklin, Massachusetts, operate a food pantry for needy people.

Some Wabanaki schools have bilingual and bicultural

Orienteering class, Micmac/Maliseet summer camp

programs, so children can learn their languages as part of their regular classes. During Motahkmiqewi Skulhawossol, National Indian Day, non-Indian children may be invited to the Indian Township school so they can learn about Wabanaki culture.

Wabanakis are reorganizing a confederacy to develop cooperation among tribal leaders and community members. Together they are working to stop factories from dumping waste into their rivers. Clean water is important for people, animals, plants, and the forests.

More facts about Wabanakis

Reservations/Communities: five reservations in Maine; communities in Massachusetts and Vermont; reserves in Canada

Total population: 10,039 (1990 census)

Some people to learn about:
Joseph Bruchac [1942–], Abenaki writer, storyteller
Mary Mitchell Gabriel [1908–], Passamaquoddy basket maker
Martin Neptune [contemporary], Penobscot photographer

Neighbors: Micmacs and Maliseets of Canada

Watching participants at the Bar Harbor Native American Festival

9

Wampanoag (womp-uh-NO-ag)

Gathering rockweed for *appanaug*, Mashpee

Choosing purple quahog (clam) shells to make wampum beads, Aquinnah

You may have heard of Martha's Vineyard and Cape Cod because many people vacation there. Have you heard of the Wampanoags, People of the First Light? There are the Aquinnah on Martha's Vineyard, the Mashpee in Cape Cod, and several other communities in Massachusetts. The Wampanoag creation story tells how Moshup, a gigantic being with great powers, made their land and taught people to live by the ocean. Every August at Aquinnah, Moshup is honored in a pageant.

Cranberries are a favorite Wampanoag food. Like many foods eaten in the United States, cranberries were first harvested by Indian peoples. The Aquinnah Wampanoags have a Cranberry Holiday in October to give thanks for the harvest.

A clambake, or *appanaug*, is a time to honor a special person or to celebrate the changing seasons. The Wampanoag gather wood, rocks, and seaweed and dig a pit. Potatoes, corn, and onions are prepared, but most

"Combing" for cranberries with a cranberry scoop, Aquinnah Cranberry Day

More facts about Wampanoags

Reservations/Communities: 480 acres of tribal land in Aquinnah, Martha's Vineyard; a community in Mashpee, Cape Cod

Total population: 1,000

Some people to learn about:
Helen Manning [1919–], Aquinnah educator, storyteller, writer
Russell Peters, [1929–2002], Mashpee tribal leader, author
Beverly Wright [contemporary], Aquinnah tribal leader

Neighbors: Narragansetts, Pequots

important are clams and quahogs, which are dug from the sea bottom. Hot rocks and seaweed go in the pit, the food is layered on top, and it's covered until it's cooked. Sample the *appanaug* at the Mashpee Powwow.

Aquinnah means "land under the hill," and the Aquinnah Wampanoags have lived there for a long time. Beauty is everywhere: the sky, the sea, and the rainbow cliffs, with 100 million years of history in them. The sacred cliffs can be seen in the unique pottery.

Wampanoag language specialist Jessie Little Doe Fermino gives language classes to Mashpee and Aquinnah tribe members. Wampanoags also try to teach their children and others how to conserve the land and not pollute. Children are taught to always leave enough fish and clams so they can reproduce. Wampanoags have had to go to court to protect their fishing rights.

You might hear of the Wampanoags when you study the first Thanksgiving in 1621. Many Wampanoags say the Pilgrims got the idea of a Thanksgiving festival from them. Indian people all over the country have harvest ceremonies to give thanks for food.

Making wampum beads from quahog shells for jewelry, Aquinnah

Haudenosaunee

(ho-dee-no-SHO-neeh)

Dressed for dancing, New York Seneca

The Haudenosaunee, which means "people of the longhouse" in the Iroquois language, are also called the League of Six Nations or the Iroquois Confederacy. There are six separate nations: Cayuga, Mohawk, Oneida, Onondaga, Seneca, and Tuscarora. Before contact with Europeans, they lived mainly in the Northeast, but now there are several Haudenosaunee communities: 10 in New York State and more in Wisconsin, Oklahoma, and Canada. Many live in cities like New York, Buffalo, and Toronto. As with the Wabanaki lands, the United States and Canadian borders separate the original Haudenosaunee homelands, but the Indian people have the right to travel back and forth. Did you know many Iroquois people have passports issued by their own Indian nations?

Haudenosaunee ancestors wisely created a democracy with a constitution called the Great Law of Peace. Every voice is heard equally—men, women, and even children. The founders of the United States were greatly influenced by this fair system and borrowed many of its ideas. The Great Law of Peace, along with other history, is recorded on wampum belts. It is now written in English, so you can read it, too.

Children can attend the Freedom School on the Akwesasne/St. Regis Mohawk Reservation. Math, reading, and writing are taught, along with the Mohawk language and culture. The school on the Wisconsin Oneida reservation is shaped like a giant turtle. Tiles on the floors and walls show Oneida history.

Helping Grandma read a story,
Wisconsin Oneida

Before the big game, Onondaga
lacrosse team

Have you ever heard of skywalkers? Many Haudeno-saunees, especially Mohawks, are called that because they are experts at building skyscrapers. The high steelworkers help build tall buildings in many cities. They helped build the World Trade Center towers in New York, and many Mohawk skywalkers helped remove debris from the buildings after they were destroyed in 2001.

Many Haudenosaunee play their traditional game of lacrosse—it is part of their religion. Although it is still a sacred game to them, its popularity has spread. Today many different people play it for sport. The Iroquois National Lacrosse Team has players from different Haudenosaunee nations and competes internationally.

More facts about Haudenosaunees

Reservations/Communities: nine reservations plus a traditional community in New York, one reservation in Wisconsin, one community in Oklahoma, and reserves in Canada

Total population: 80,822

Some people to learn about:
Ray Fadden [1910–], Mohawk cultural teacher, historian, writer
Richard Hill [1950–], Tuscarora artist, museum curator, photographer
Joanne Shenandoah [contemporary], Oneida singer, actor

Neighbors: Ramapough in New Jersey, Mohegan and Schaghticoke in Connecticut

Learning the history of a wampum belt from Chief Oren Lyons, Onondaga

Powhatan (POW-hah-tan)

A pottery demonstration at a festival, Mattaponi

Playing with a bird friend, Rappahannock

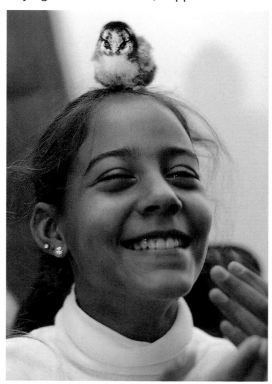

Did you know that Pocahontas was an ancestor of the present-day Powhatan people? The Powhatans of Virginia, named after one of their great chiefs, live in the same place Pocahontas did centuries ago. The Powhatan Confederacy used to include many different peoples, but today there are only a few groups, including the Pamunkey, Mattaponi, Nansemond, Chickahominy, and Rappahannock. After Europeans arrived in the Western Hemisphere, life became difficult for Native peoples. Powhatans were one of the first groups to experience loss of lives, land, food, health, and culture.

Only the Pamunkey and the Mattaponi have reservations. They are located in scenic and rural river valleys. Rivers are important to them; they own and operate hatcheries to protect the shad fish so the fish can reproduce. Watching the fishermen catch the shad is fun! They take them to the hatchery, a nursery for fish, so the eggs can be cared for in a safe place. After the eggs hatch and the fish get bigger, they are released into the river. Powhatans are knowledgeable about river ecology and teach others how to conserve natural river habitats, too.

The Pamunkey are fantastic potters. They gather clay from the same clay bed their ancestors did over 400 years ago. Digging for it is like getting to play in mud, but for a purpose. But it's a lot of work digging and preparing clay; usually the grown-ups do it. Children learn the process from their elders. There is a school where non-Powhatans can learn, too. Many of the vases, bowls, and plates have stories about the Pamunkey people on them and are collectors' items.

Pottery making is not all Powhatan children learn. Dance, medicine, food, beadworking, and other parts of the culture are taught by older people. Although the Powhatan had most of their land taken, they maintain a strong presence in Virginia. Visit the Pamunkey Indian Museum or the Mattaponi Marine Science Center to learn more about the Powhatan culture.

Powhatan people often move to places like Pennsylvania, New Jersey, and Maryland, but they still keep in contact with one another. Events like the Chickahominy Fall Festival bring everyone together. Powhatan people travel to other Indian communities to participate in powwows and festivals.

In a 1646 treaty with Virginia's colonial government, Mattaponi and Pamunkey leaders agreed to deliver fresh game and fish to the Virginia government every year. To this day they keep their word.

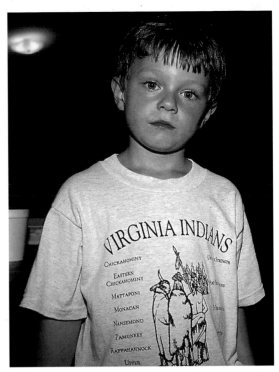

Proud of his heritage, Nansemond

More facts about Powhatans

Reservations/Communities: two reservations and several communities in Virginia

Total population: 2,879 (1990 census)

Some people to learn about:
Muriel Miguel [contemporary], Rappahannock founder, Spider Woman's Theater
Linwood Custalow [1937–], Mattaponi tribal leader, physician
Jack D. Forbes [1934–], Rappahannock author, university professor

Neighbors: Powhatan Renapes of New Jersey

Relaxing in a recreated Powhatan historical dwelling at Jamestown, Virginia

15

Lumbee (LUM-bee)

Enjoying Lumbee Homecoming

Playing on the steps of Old Main, University of North Carolina at Pembroke

The Lumbees are named after the Lumber River, which flows through the center of their community. The river is the heartbeat of the people. They like to fish and canoe on it. The Lumbees, who live in southeast North Carolina, are the largest tribe east of the Mississippi River. Land is privately, not tribally, owned and the Lumbees do not have a reservation.

Almost everyone comes home in July for Lumbee Homecoming, even if they live in Detroit or Baltimore. There are parades, powwows, dancing, singing, art shows, and beauty pageants. There is a Miss Lumbee contest; the winner spends the year representing Lumbees around the country.

Singing is a traditional part of Lumbee lives. Many churches in Lumbee land give children the opportunity to participate in different choirs. They are very talented gospel singers. The churches are places to meet friends for youth activities. They provide special events and groups for elders, too.

The elders teach time-honored crafts like Lumbee patchwork. A favorite pattern is the Long Leaf Pinecone—there are blankets, rugs, and clothing with this beautiful design.

Over 100 years ago, the Lumbee started a teacher training school. Today it is called the University of North Carolina at Pembroke and is a college for non-Indians, too. Lumbees also own farms and businesses and work in many different jobs. Children help on the farms and get to ride and take care of the horses.

In the schools, most of the children are Lumbee. They like sports and have baseball and basketball teams. The tribe has day care centers and a Head Start program.

A Lumbee ambassador,
Lumbee Homecoming

A quiet moment on the banks
of the Lumber River

More facts about Lumbees

Reservations/Communities: one
    community in Pembroke, North Carolina

Total population: 57,868

Some people to learn about:
Donna Chavis [contemporary], consultant
    to North Carolina Commission of
    Indian Affairs
Jana (Sampson) Lumbee [1979–], pop
    musician
Arlinda Locklear [1951–], attorney

Neighbors: Cherokees, Coharies, Haliwa-
    Saponis, Meherrins

Did you know there was a Lumbee Robin Hood? His name was Henry Berry Lowrie, and he fought for the rights of poor people everywhere. He protected Indian people and others whose land was being taken over by white settlers in the 1800s.

Lumbee children are taught to be fair, just, and strong. In fact, in 1958 the Lumbees chased away the Ku Klux Klan, a hate group, without anyone getting injured. The Klan was planning to hold a rally to scare Indians. The KKK learned to stay out of Lumbee country.

Celebrating at a
Lumbee wedding

Choctaw (CHOCK-tah)

Carrying a swamp cane basket at the Choctaw Fair

Getting the feel of the *kabocca*

Eastern Mississippi is home to the Mississippi Choctaws. In the 1800s the United States government forced many Choctaws to move to Oklahoma, along with other tribes. The United States wanted Choctaw land for white settlers. At one time the Choctaws lived in Alabama, Georgia, and Louisiana, too.

Have you heard of the Code Talkers? Choctaw was one of the first Indian languages used in World War I to send secret messages for the U.S. Army. The enemy never figured it out, and the Choctaw soldiers were honored for their contribution. Choctaw language is still very important to the Choctaw people, who work hard to protect it from extinction.

There are language programs in schools, and language classes are part of summer camps. Besides learning Choctaw, students learn how to design Web pages. Many kids like using the digital camera and image-editing software the best. Students put lots of information about Choctaws on the Web, including the Choctaw Fair.

The Choctaw Fair is a weeklong event held every July. There are pageants, cultural exhibits, Choctaw social dancers from each community, rides, entertainers, and tons of visitors from all over. You can have traditional food like *holhponi*, or fresh hominy. Visitors can see Choctaw artists make their famous swampcane baskets in the museum, or attend the Stickball World Series.

Did you know that Indian stickball is an official part of the Mississippi State Games? Stickball is a hard game

A fast and furious game of stickball

to play; it's something like lacrosse with no protective gear. The *towa* and *kabocca*, stickball equipment, have to be handmade, and the game has more rules today than it did long ago. Choctaw kids also play many other sports and have a basketball and soccer camp.

There is a lot of activity on the Choctaw reservations. The nation has one of the largest casinos and hotels in the South. People come to play on the Dancing Rabbit golf courses. The forestry and environmental programs keep the Choctaw reservations in good shape for the nation and guests.

More facts about Choctaws

Reservations/Communities: one reservation each in Louisiana and Mississippi; one community in Oklahoma

Total population: 158,774

Some people to learn about:
Owanah Anderson [1926–], Oklahoma Episcopal Church leader, women's rights activist
Phil Lucas [contemporary], Oklahoma film producer, director
Philip Martin [1926–], Mississippi tribal leader

Neighbors: Poarch Band of Creeks, Chitimachas, Tunica-Biloxis

Lining up on graduation day

Seminole (SEM-eh-nole)

Learning beading at Ahfachkee Elementary School, Big Cypress

Beautiful patchwork clothing at the annual Hollywood powwow

Have you been to Walt Disney World in Florida? You should visit the Seminole recreation park called the Billie Swamp Safari. You get to ride in swamp buggies and airboats and see Everglades animals like alligators. The Seminole Tribe has six reservations in southern Florida—Big Cypress, Brighton, Hollywood, Fort Pierce, Tampa, and Immokalee. The U.S. government forced many Seminoles to relocate to Oklahoma in the 1800s. Today there are 14 Seminole communities in the east central part of Oklahoma.

Some Seminole communities are in the Everglades, home to endangered species like the Florida panther. Seminoles try to protect the Everglades and its unique wildlife. Ancestors of the Seminoles came from Georgia and northern Florida, fleeing from white settlers who took their land. They went deeper into Florida's swamps, learning to survive and thrive in a different environment. Today many Seminoles live in urban areas near Miami and Tampa.

Seminole youth are honored at a sports banquet for baseball, basketball, football, karate, volleyball, rodeo events, T-ball, and even bowling. Most kids attend public schools with non-Indians, but on the Big Cypress Reservation, they learn Seminole culture and other subjects in an all-Indian school. The school won the federal Distinguished School Award. Field trips are really fun—one time the children flew in their tribal jet to Cape Canaveral for a tour of NASA!

Seminoles manufacture a small aircraft called an acrobatic sports plane. Some reservations have large commercial produce farms, and some raise cattle.

Getting a ride at Big Cypress

Another way for Seminole people to earn a living is in the tourist industry. People from around the world visit their casinos, campgrounds, restaurants, nature trails, and swamps. On the Big Cypress Reservation's Ah-Tah-Thi-Ki Museum, which means "place to learn," visitors get a glimpse of historic and present-day Seminole life. There are festivals, rodeos, and concerts, too.

On special occasions, Seminoles wear unique outfits made of patchwork, tiny pieces of colorful cloth sewn into patterns. Before Seminoles had electricity, they made their world-famous clothing with hand-cranked sewing machines. Today, collectors can buy Seminole dolls dressed in patchwork.

More facts about Seminoles

Reservations/Communities: six Seminole reservations in Florida; 14 communities in Oklahoma

Total population: 27,431

Some people to learn about:
Alice Brown Davis [1852–1935], Oklahoma tribal leader
Kelley Haney [contemporary], Oklahoma state senator and sculptor
Betty Mae Tiger Jumper [1923–], Florida tribal leader

Neighbors: Miccosukees in Florida

Wrestling an alligator at Hollywood

Ojibway

(o-JIB-way)

Picking blueberries, Grand Portage

Collecting sap to make maple syrup,
Grand Portage

Anishinabe is the original name of the people called Ojibway, Chippewa, or Ojibwe. Their reservations are located in Michigan, Minnesota, Montana, North Dakota, and Wisconsin. Many Ojibway live in big cities like Minneapolis. Their communities are known for their forests and crystal clear lakes. Thousands of years ago, the Sokaogon Chippewa settled in Wisconsin's Mole Lake area and found wild rice growing on the water. Today they struggle to keep the mining industry from polluting their lake and killing their rice and fish.

Have you ever eaten *manoomin*? That's the Ojibway word for wild rice. It is harvested from rivers and lakes by canoe. Some families continue the ricing tradition together, careful to protect future harvests of *manoomin*. Native Harvest, a store operated by the White Earth Land Recovery Project on Minnesota's White Earth Reservation, sells hand-harvested *manoomin* and other Ojibway-grown foods like maple syrup, hominy, and wild rice pancake mix.

Trees, rivers, and lakes are vital to most Ojibway communities, and fishing is a big part of life. Reservations like Red Lake in Minnesota operate fish hatcheries to keep the fish population healthy and plentiful. Although treaties provide the Ojibway people fishing rights, some legislators, fishermen, and other non-Ojibways have tried to take these rights away, resulting in legal battles.

Did you know that the Ojibway language is listed in the Guinness Book of World Records? It has over 6,000 verb forms, while English has fewer than 20. School programs and culture camps teach the language.

Many people like to visit Ojibway country to ski, snowmobile, hike, canoe, ice fish, play golf, camp, attend powwows, and tour museums on the many reservations. Some parents work for the nations' tourist businesses, and others work for Ojibway clinics, schools, factories, sawmills, fish hatcheries, and tribal governments.

Making and playing flutes, Leech Lake

More facts about Ojibways

Reservations/Communities: seven reservations each in Minnesota, Michigan, and Wisconsin; one reservation each in North Dakota and Montana, and reserves in Canada

Total population: 149,669

Some people to learn about:
Louise Erdrich [1954–], North Dakota Turtle Mountain poet, novelist
Earl Nyholm [contemporary], Michigan Keweenaw canoe maker, linguist
Keith Secola [1957–], Minnesota Bois Forte musician

Neighbors: Crees, Dakotas, Ho-Chunks, Menominees, Oneidas, Ottawas, Potawatomis

Did you know that Winona LaDuke from the White Earth Reservation ran for vice president of the United States twice? She also founded the White Earth Land Recovery Project, which has bought back hundreds of acres of land and operates horse riding programs for kids.

Wild ricing with poet Jim Northrup, Fond du Lac

Meskwaki (meh-SQUAWK-ee)

Keeping an eye on the corral during the powwow

Dressing up in regalia for Proclamation Day

Proclamation Day is the Meskwaki national holiday in July, when Meskwakis celebrate their return to Iowa almost 150 years ago. Their ancestors were forced out of Iowa, but returned and bought the very land where they live today. The Meskwakis, People of the Red Earth, live on the only reservation in Iowa, a community of rolling meadows and woodlands of pine, maple, and walnut trees.

Meskwaki children look forward to the ceremonies, games, dancing, and feasting that connect them to the past. Right after Proclamation Day, they start getting ready for the big powwow in August. Squash, corn, and beans are harvested and dried, traditional outfits are completed, and wickiups are erected.

Do you know what a wickiup is? It's the Meskwaki dome-shaped house. Canvas covers the sapling frame. Architects say that it's one of the strongest structures of its kind! For four days during the powwow, kids and their families get to sleep in wickiups on the powwow grounds. It's fun hanging out with friends and relatives, dancing, singing, listening to storytelling, and eating traditional foods.

Meskwakis are considered bilingual: almost everyone speaks Meskwaki and English. Adeline Wanatee, a former chief, is a Meskwaki language and resource specialist for the Smithsonian. Meskwaki dancers have learned different foreign phrases on their travels to places like the Netherlands. It's great to be able to speak more than one language.

Tradition is all around the Meskwakis. The new school in Tama was built with Meskwaki culture in mind. There are domes fashioned like wickiups, Meskwaki designs in the tiles, and greenery everywhere so that students can be part of the natural world. It is a beautiful place to study Meskwaki language and culture, along with other subjects like math and science.

History is a favorite subject. The Meskwaki Bingo-Casino-Hotel has a History Wall for visitors to learn, too. Many parents work for the nation in the casino or in tribal offices. Famous people like Shaggy and Willie Nelson have performed at the casino. There's always something exciting happening right there in the middle of the Iowa cornfields.

Piggybacking during a powwow break

More facts about Meskwakis

Reservations/Communities: one reservation in Iowa; a community in Oklahoma (Sac and Fox)

Total population: 1,279 (1990 census)

Some people to learn about:
Adeline Wanatee [1910–], political activist, language educator
Don Wanatee [contemporary], political activist
Ray Young Bear [1950–], poet

Neighbors: Kickapoos, Potawatomis

Ready for a dance performance

Cherokee (CHAIR-oh-kee)

Putting on turtle shell rattles

Making a honeysuckle vine basket

O*siyo* is how to say hello in Cherokee land in northeastern Oklahoma. Cherokees are the largest Indian tribe in Oklahoma. Their hilly country is dotted with soybeans and wheat farms.

For centuries, before the Europeans came, the Cherokees occupied a large area in the Southeast. In the 1800s Americans wanted Cherokee homelands, rich with farms and gold deposits. In a famous legal battle, the Cherokees took their case to the Supreme Court and won. But the government at the time did not support the Cherokee Nation; federal and state troops forced most of them to leave their homes. They had to walk all the way to Oklahoma in snow and ice with hardly any food or clothing. That was called the Trail of Tears, because the Cherokee lost everything, and thousands died on the

way. Today there are still Cherokees in North Carolina and other southeastern states; their ancestors escaped the Trail.

Tribal offices and the Cherokee Heritage Center are located in the Cherokee capital, Tahlequah, Oklahoma. The Heritage Center has a library, museum, amphitheater, and a replica of an ancient village. In September there is a weeklong Cherokee holiday with a parade, rodeo, powwow, traditional games, and feasting. Performers like Wes Studi come home for the holidays, and the chief gives a State of the Nation speech, which is covered by the media. You may have heard of the Cherokee chief Wilma Mankiller, who led the Oklahoma Cherokees from 1985 to 1995.

The Cherokee alphabet, or syllabary, is taught in schools. Computer language programs help students learn it better. Did you know that the *Cherokee Advocate*, printed in English and Cherokee, was the first newspaper in the state of Oklahoma?

Cherokee young people play all kinds of sports and learn how to make Cherokee baskets, quilts, ribbon shirts, and tear dresses, their national outfits. Parents work in a variety of jobs and businesses, many of them tribally owned, like the pine-tree production project, which promotes replanting to help the environment. Cherokees like to get together as families and go to a ball game, a traditional stomp dance, church, or a hog-fry. Whatever they do, children are taught to be in harmony and balance.

More facts about Cherokees

Reservations/Communities: one reservation in North Carolina, communities in 14 Oklahoma counties, and communities in Mississippi, Tennessee, Virginia, and Georgia

Total population: 729,533

Some people to learn about:
Will Rogers [1879–1935], Oklahoma humorist, writer, actor
Gelvin Stevenson, [1943–], Oklahoma economist
Eddie Swimmer [contemporary], North Carolina hoop dancer, storyteller

Neighbors: Catawbas in South Carolina; Creeks, Eastern Shawnees, Miamis, Modocs, Ottawas, Quapaws, Seneca-Cayugas, and Wyandottes in Oklahoma

Listening to an elder's stories, Okay, Oklahoma

27

Comanche (ka-MAN-shee)

Waiting for the dance to begin, Comanche Homecoming Powwow

Competing in the traditional dance category, Comanche Homecoming Powwow

Some say the Comanches of Oklahoma are the greatest horse riders in America. Their ancestors, called Lords of the Plains, trained and traded horses from North Dakota to Mexico. Did you know that Comanche riders could hold on with their feet around the mustang's neck while galloping? The Comanches used to own thousands of horses. To prevent Comanches from defending their homelands, the U.S. Army killed most of their horses in the 1800s.

Today Comanches still love horses and own many ranches around tribal headquarters near Lawton, Oklahoma. Programs and summer day camps teach children to ride and to take care of the special mustangs. Medicine Hat and War Bonnet mustangs are breeds the Comanches developed. Horses need good, clean land, so the Comanche Environmental Protection Agency protects their territory from polluters.

Besides horseback riding, Comanche young people compete in all kinds of sports, especially the ones that have a lot of running. Many excel in track, football, and basketball, and often win awards in school team sports. During the Comanche Nation Fair, competitions range from running to throwing horseshoes.

Sports are a big part of Comanche children's lives, but they are expected to do well in school, too. Comanches, like other Native Americans, consider education very important. There are special programs where children study the Comanche language. It is said that the largest percentage of Indian students enrolled in college are Comanches.

Special programs teach Comanche sign language, history, dancing, manners, art, and much more. Comanche outfits are prized for their beautiful beadwork and feather work. Children learn how to make the clothing, which is worn on special occasions like powwows. They also learn how to do the Buffalo, Snake, and other dances.

Many Comanches own private businesses, but the casino and some other enterprises belong to everyone in the nation. Some parents work on the Fort Sill military base. Many Comanches live in Texas, New Mexico, and California. In July everyone comes home for Comanche Homecoming. It's a happy time with powwows, foods like *atawaska* (a dried corn dish), singing, games, and, of course, the wonderful mustangs. If you attend the Homecoming, you can see that the Comanches are still the Lords of the Plains.

Winning ribbons in an English-style jumping competition

More facts about Comanches

Reservations/Communities: one community in Oklahoma

Total population: 19,376

Some people to learn about:
Charles Chibitty [1921–], Code Talker
LaDonna Harris [1931–], political activist
Cornel Pewewardy [1952–], educator, singer

Neighbors: Apaches, Caddos, Delawares, Kiowas, Wichitas

Riding in the Comanche Nation Fair Parade dressed in Southern Straight traditional regalia

Lakota (lah-COE-tah)

Resting with horse friends at the Bigfoot Memorial Ride, Pine Ridge Reservation

Taking an ice-cream break, Rosebud Reservation

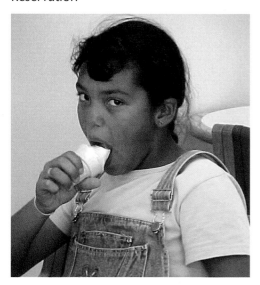

The Lakotas are from the Cheyenne River, Crow Creek, Lower Brulé, Pine Ridge, and Rosebud reservations in South Dakota, and the Standing Rock Reservation that sits on both sides of the border between North and South Dakota. They are often referred to as the Sioux. Their landscape includes rolling hills, buttes, prairie, badlands, mountains, and rivers.

Lakotas were brilliant soldiers who defended their land well. Most people have heard of the Lakota spiritual leader Sitting Bull (1831–1890). Sitting Bull College on the Standing Rock Reservation and three other Lakota colleges offer not only education, but community programs as well.

Lakota children stay in tipis only on special occasions like powwows or ceremonies. There are community programs where children study Lakota culture and also bowl, swim, or play midnight basketball.

Many Native people are struggling to get back the Black Hills, or Paha Sapa in the Lakota language. They were taken illegally by the U.S. government. The Paha Sapa are as sacred to the Lakota as other people's churches, synagogues, or mosques. The Lakota pray and have ceremonies there. Camp Paha Sapa gives Lakota young people from urban and reservation communities an opportunity to attend camp in the Black Hills and study Lakota culture.

Many Lakotas are known for long-distance running. In 1964 Billy Mills from Pine Ridge became the only American to win Olympic gold in a 10,000-meter race.

Fishing with corn kernels, Rosebud Reservation

Today Mr. Mills's program, Running Strong for American Indian Youth, sponsors different youth activities in Lakota communities, like the Organic Gardens and the youth centers. Horseback riding and rodeo competitions are favorite activities, too. Lakota people are also known for being great artists. Their paintings, sculptures, and quilts can be seen in many museums.

Tribal governments, casinos, farms, schools, craft businesses, and buffalo and cattle ranches employ Lakota people. On the Cheyenne River Reservation, Lakotas have reintroduced the black-footed ferret, one of the most endangered mammals in the United States. The Prairie Management Program plans to restore the vanishing prairie ecosystem. On the Pine Ridge Reservation, the Oglala Sioux Parks and Recreation Authority manages the tribe's fisheries and wildlife resources and oversees the buffalo program.

Miss Paha Sapa, Pine Ridge Reservation

More facts about Lakotas

Reservations/Communities: five reservations in South Dakota; one reservation in North and South Dakota

Total population: 107,400

Some people to learn about:
Tim Giago [1934–], Pine Ridge Lakota publisher, journalist
Ben Reifel [1906–1990], Rosebud Lakota U.S. congressman
Virginia Driving Hawk Sneve [1933–], Rosebud Lakota children's book writer

Neighbors: Arikaras, Dakotas, Hidatsas, Mandans, Nakotas

Dancing with the wind, Lower Brulé Reservation in South Dakota

Crow (KROWE)

Gathering at the Tipi Capital of the World, Crow Fair

"Horsing around" at the Crow Fair Rodeo

Hundreds of tipis reach for the sky in the Tipi Capital of the World. It's not on a television show, but on the Crow reservation in Montana, every August during Crow Fair. In the Crow language, the name for the people is *Apsáalooke*, which means "children of the long-beaked bird." A long time ago, the Hidatsa people, who were Crow relatives, were trying to explain the tribe's name to the white explorers in sign language. When they made the motion of a bird flapping his wings, the white people started calling them Crow!

You can learn more about Crows during Crow Fair. It takes two weeks to set up all those tipis. The fun begins with a big parade. People on horseback, Miss Crow Fair in a convertible, and drum groups on floats wave at the spectators. Indian people from as far away as Mexico join the celebration. You can see traditional outfits, which are beaded with beautiful designs of geometrics and flowers.

Even horse gear is beaded, so the horses can look beautiful, too.

After the parade there are powwows, horse racing, rodeos, giveaways, games, and feasting. It is a great time for Crow children to camp out and visit with friends and family.

Learning history from an elder at Lodge Grass

Crow Fair only happens once a year. The rest of the time, Crow people live in houses, not tipis, and attend reservation schools. Some also attend Little Big Horn College, directed for years by Janine Pease Pretty On Top. The Battle of Little Big Horn took place on Crow land.

Family is very important to the Crow—the clan is an extended family. Montana state senator Bill Yellowtail asked for his clan's advice and approval before he ran for elected office.

Crow homelands have high plains and mountains and lots of natural resources like coal and oil. Much of the reservation is leased to mining companies and ranchers. One of the largest buffalo herds in Indian country is located on the Crow reservation. Tribal members help other tribes start or enlarge their buffalo herds.

Riding a mechanical bucking bronco, Crow Fair Rodeo

The Crow word for buffalo is *bi'shee*. Many Crow people can speak both English and Crow. By speaking their own language, Crow people keep their traditions even stronger.

Some parents work for the tribal hospital, visitors center, tribal office, or in the schools. They have jobs as social workers, policemen, or teachers. Every adult in the Crow nation is on the tribal council—a real democracy.

More facts about Crows

Reservations/Communities: one reservation in Montana

Total population: 13,394

Some people to learn about:
Gregory W. Frazier [1947–], motorcycle adventurer, writer
Joseph Medicine Crow [1913–], tribal historian
Kevin Red Star [1943–], painter

Neighbors: Blackfeet, Chippewa-Crees, Gros Ventres, Northern Cheyennes, Salish-Kootenais

Nez Perce (NEZ purse)

Videotaping the Young Horseman Project

Dressed for a powwow at Wallowa

ee-mee-poo, the real name of the Nez Perce, means "the people." According to tradition, explorers Lewis and Clark named the tribe's ancestors *Nez Perce*, which means "pierced nose" in French—but the tribe never pierced their noses! Rivers, valleys, mountains, forests, and high prairies make up Nez Perce land in north central Idaho.

Have you heard of the Appaloosa (*Akahl-teke*) horse? Centuries ago, the Nez Perce developed the breed and had the largest horse herd in North America. In the 1800s white settlers, miners, and the U.S. government killed the horses and took over much of the original Nez Perce homelands in Oregon, forcing them onto a tiny reservation in Idaho. In 1877 Chief Joseph, hoping to avoid conflicts, tried to lead his people to safety in Canada. For 115 days the U. S. Army chased the Nez Perce over 1,400 miles of harsh Montana terrain in wintry weather before they were able to capture them. Historians declared this one of the most brilliant retreats in history.

Nez Perce youth can join a special program called "In the Saddle on the Nez Perce Trail," riding the same difficult route their ancestors did as they fled from soldiers in 1877. They learn backcountry camping and improve their riding skills. Although they have a lot of comforts that their ancestors did not have, the route is a hard one to follow. It makes Nez Perce kids appreciate the hardships their ancestors had on this same trail.

Today the Nez Perce are bringing back the Appaloosa and have a special program that makes sure the breed is

Grooming an Appaloosa horse

strong and healthy. The Young Horsemen Project teaches children all about horses. Not only do they learn how to improve their horsemanship, but they are also taught how to manage the horse business. Horses need a lot of care and special foods. During the school year, kids play sports and study, and continue to learn Nez Perce ways.

Parents may farm, work for the tribal government, or work in the casino. Chinook salmon swim up Nez Perce rivers to spawn; fishing is important to the tribe. The Nez Perce work hard to protect the land.

More facts about Nez Perces

Reservations/Communities: one reservation in Idaho; Nez Perces also live on the Colville Reservation in Washington State

Total population: 3,250

Some people to learn about:
Doug Hyde [1946–], sculptor
Hattie Kaufman [contemporary], television reporter
Jackson Sundown [1863–1923], rodeo champion

Neighbors: Coeur d'Alenes, Colvilles, Kootenais, Spokanes, Umatillas

Caring for a kitten

Shoshone (sha-SHO-nee)

Getting dance pointers from a powwow video, Fort Washakie, Wyoming

The Shoshones have communities in California, Idaho, Nevada, Utah, and Wyoming. Landscapes are varied and include grazing lands, high deserts, mountains, and forests. The Lone Pine Reservation in California is near the tallest mountain in the continental United States, Mount Whitney.

Activist sisters Carrie and Mary Dann, of the Western Shoshone Nation in Nevada, lead the struggle to preserve their 24-million-acre homeland. The land has been damaged by logging, strip mining, oil drilling, and nuclear testing. They've even gone to Geneva, Switzerland, to present the case to the world court and show how the Shoshone treaties are being broken. Corbin Harney, also an elder, travels around the world teaching the dangers of nuclear warfare. The Western Shoshone Nation is considered the most bombed nation in the world, because the United States government has detonated more than 800 bombs on their land.

Elders also make sure the Shoshone language is preserved and schools are bilingual. Shoshone beadwork and porcupine quillwork are some of the best and can be purchased through tribal stores like the Clothes Horse on the Fort Hall Reservation in Idaho. You can see Shoshone outfits at events like Shoshone Days at Wind River, Wyoming's only Indian reservation. Rodeos, powwows, races, and parades are all part of the festivities.

Shoshones raise buffalo and cattle. On the Fort Hall reservation, you can enjoy a Shoshone meal of buffalo steak and read the *Sho-Ban Tribal Newspaper* in the Oregon Trail Restaurant. You can visit Shoshone museums or read books by Shoshone historians Ned

Snack time, Fort Washakie, Wyoming

Setting up a tipi, Fort Washakie, Wyoming

Blackhawk or Steven Crum to learn more. When you think of the Shoshone, remember *shundahai*, which means "peace and harmony with all creation."

Checking out the Mars Rover prototype, Duck Water Shoshone, Nevada

More facts about Shoshones

Reservations/Communities: 12 reservations in Nevada, one in Utah, one in Idaho, one in Wyoming, and four in California

Total population: 12,026

Some people to learn about:
Randy'L He-Dow Teton [1976–], Idaho Shoshone model for Sacajawea coin
Laine Thom [1952–], Utah Shoshone artist, author
Mark Trahant [1957–], Idaho Shoshone journalist

Neighbors: Arapahos, Bannocks, Goshutes, Paiutes, Washoes

Havasupai (HAV-ah-SOUP-eye)

Horses are a great way to get around in Supai, Arizona

Hello from Supai!

Hello! Hello! It really echoes in the beautiful Havasupai canyons, located at the bottom of the Grand Canyon. In the Havasupai language, the people call themselves *Havasuw Baaja*, which means "people of the blue-green waters."

The Havasupai waterfalls and river do have blue-green water, fresh and clean. Their village, called Supai, is surrounded by steep red-rock walls. People from around the world like to visit, but they have to make plans months ahead.

See, you cannot get there by boat, train, car, or plane. You can only reach Supai by helicopter, or by walking or riding a horse down a steep eight-mile trail. The Havasupai operate campsites and a lodge where tourists can stay, but there is limited space. There are no paved roads, cars, or movie theaters, and only one store. Havasupai people who own cars park them in Hilltop and walk down, too. Three waterfalls in the canyon are sacred to the Havasupai. One of them, Havasu Falls, spills 125 feet down into an azure-colored circular pool.

Did you know that pack-mule trains deliver the Havasupais' mail? They have the only post office in the United States that gets its mail delivered by animals! Televisions, computers, clothes, and groceries, along with regular mail, are all strapped onto the animals and carried down the trails. The mail comes daily, even in winter. Some parents work for the post office. Others work in the tourist lodge and restaurant, tribal government office, health clinic, and school.

Havasupais are fortunate to speak their own language.

Dressed in traditional regalia in front of canyon walls

Learning about the dangers of uranium mining from Carletta Tilousi

More facts about Havasupais

Reservations/Communities: one reservation in Arizona

Total population: 1,000

Some people to learn about:
Carletta Tilousi [1970–], anti-uranium mining activist
Rex Tilousi [1947–], tribal leader
James Uqualla [contemporary], tribal leader

Neighbors: Hopis, Hualapais, Mojaves, Navajos

In school, they learn English, too. The Havasupai school goes to eighth grade; then children attend boarding school in California or public high schools where they may stay during the school year. Many people now have Internet service, so older brothers and sisters can e-mail home every day. That helps when they get homesick. The annual Peach Festival is usually held in Supai in late August, when the high school kids are home. There are many different activities, from basketball to dancing to the local reggae band.

Land and water are sacred to the Havasupai, and they are careful to take care of them. Mining companies would like to take out the uranium found deep inside the land. But Havasupais want to protect the environment from the pollution caused by mining.

At Hilltop, where the road to Supai begins

Navajo (NAV-a-hoe)

Using three modes of transportation at Monument Valley on the Arizona-Utah border

Y*a'at' eeh* means "hello" in the Navajo language. The Navajo Nation, the largest reservation in the United States, is located in New Mexico, Utah, and Arizona. Canyons, mesas, alpine forests, and deserts make up the reservation, larger than the state of West Virginia. There are pretty names for places, like Painted Desert and Rainbow Bridge. Did you know that the Navajo name for themselves is *Dine?* It means "the people."

The Navajo capital is Window Rock, Arizona. Just like the federal government, the Navajo Nation has three branches. The court system includes Peacemaker courts, operated in a traditional Navajo way. Many people speak Navajo and practice time-honored ways of handling disputes.

Navajo language and culture are usually taught in school along with academic subjects. Some children have to take a bus a long way to get to school. Homes are usually far from schools and neighbors, because many Navajos have sheep which need a lot of space to graze. The children help with the sheep, and the dogs are smart about taking care of the sheep, too!

The sheep provide plenty of wool for the famous Navajo blankets and rugs. They take a long time to make. Weavers shear the sheep, spin the wool into yarn, ready the loom, make dyes, color the wool, and then it's time to begin weaving. The patterns come from the weaver's head and heart. Most weavers start as young girls—it's a good way to learn patience. Did you know

Sharing a laugh with Mom

Shepherding at Red Mesa, Utah

that no two rugs are ever exactly alike?

Some parents earn a living by weaving, but others are employed in government jobs, computer-part manufacturing, tourism, and farming. Produce with the Navajo Pride label is grown right on the reservation. Mining companies employ people, too, but many Navajos are saddened by what the strip mining does to the land.

In the 1860s, Navajos were forced to leave their homelands and walk over 300 miles to a New Mexico fort, where they were imprisoned for four years. Thousands died on the "Long Walk." Navajos won the right to return to their home, where they live today.

More facts about Navajos

Reservations/Communities: one large reservation in Arizona, New Mexico, and Utah; three small reservations in New Mexico

Total population: 298,197

Some people to learn about:
Lori Arviso Alvord [1958–], surgeon
Notah Begay III [1972–], championship golfer
Annie Dodge Wauneka [1910–1997], health educator

Neighbors: Apaches, Havasupais, Hopis, Pimas, Tohono O'odhams

Little Miss Four Corners at the Navajo Fair, Window Rock, Arizona

Fun at the school playground, Ganada, Arizona

Pueblo (PWEH-blow)

Corn dancing at San Juan

Twenty different Pueblos in New Mexico and Arizona are crunched into these two pages! They are the Acoma, Cochiti, Hopi, Isleta, Jemez, Laguna, Nambe, Picuris, Pojoaque, Sandia, San Felipe, San Ildefonso, San Juan, Santa Ana, Santa Clara, Santo Domingo, Taos, Tesuque, Zia, and Zuni. When the Spanish invaded the Southwest in the 1500s, they called these groups *pueblos*, the Spanish word for towns. Although the Pueblo people live in two different states and speak different languages, the name Pueblo stuck and they all get grouped together.

Like the Pueblo peoples, the lands are different, too. Some communities like the Nambe (People of the Round Earth) Pueblo have waterfalls, mountains, and lakes, while the Santa Ana Pueblo is dry and flat.

The Cochiti Pueblo has a beautiful lake marina where people can play all kinds of water sports. Its golf course is rated one of the best. Cochitis, like many other Pueblo peoples, are famous for their pottery. Artist Helen Cordero was the first to design the popular storyteller figure, a clay sculpture that shows a grandfather sitting with many children while he tells his story to them.

People earn a living at farming, ranching, and piñon nut harvesting. Some are scientists, lawyers, engineers, or tribal government workers. The Laguna Pueblo operates a communication products factory. The Pojoaque (Water Drinking Place) Pueblo has a race track. Pueblo people also make and sell pottery, baskets, and their world-famous silver jewelry, too. Artwork is often a family project, with everyone helping out.

The Pueblo peoples have been known throughout history as great farmers. In the San Juan Pueblo are the Ohkay T'owa gardens, which means "the People of San Juan's" gardens. This is an agricultural cooperative where people

Playing in the snow at Laguna

Climbing ancient stairs at Acoma

get together to raise native foods like corn, beans, squash, and melons. A "living classroom" teaches traditional and modern farming methods that protect the environment and work in harmony with nature. Running is also a Pueblo tradition—many Pueblo people have set records in track and field events.

Some Pueblo communities invite the public to their ceremonies and feast days. People who attend are asked to be silent and respectful.

More facts about Pueblos

Reservations/Communities: 19 Pueblos in New Mexico; one Pueblo in Arizona

Total population: 74,085

Some people to learn about:
Simon Ortiz [1941–], Acoma poet
Beverly R. Singer [1954–], Santa Clara filmmaker, educator
Verna Williamson-Teller [1951–], Isleta tribal leader

Neighbors: Apaches, Havasupais, Navajos

Golfing at Cochiti

Cross-country running at Zuni

43

Cahuilla (kha-WE-yah)

Hearing amazing tales at the California Indian Storytelling Association peformance

The Native people of the California desert, canyons, and mountains are the Kha-we-yah, or as the Spanish called them, the Cahuillas. There are ten bands of Kha-we-yah: Agua Caliente, Augustine, Cabazon, Los Coyotes, Cahuilla, Morongo, Santa Rosa, Soboba, Ramona, and Torres-Martinez. The reservations may be different, but many Cahuillas have similar traditions, like the famous Bird Songs.

Bird Songs tell the story of the Cahuilla people all the way back to the Ice Age. The songs and dances show how the people went through hardships. Rattles, their musical instruments, are made very carefully from gourds. The rattle sounds tell the dancers how to move. The Cahuilla Bird Singers share their songs and dances with non-Cahuillas so that others can understand Cahuilla traditions.

If you speak Spanish, you probably know that *agua caliente* means "hot water." For centuries, the Agua Caliente Cahuilla have been lucky enough to have warm mineral springs. People from all over the world visit their spa in Palm Springs to relax in the healing waters.

There are many reasons people like to come to Cahuilla reservations. They visit the Agua Caliente Reservation to go horseback riding in its beautiful canyons. The canyons have the greatest concentration of wild desert palm trees in the world. Hollywood is always filming movies in the Cahuillas' backyard! Tourists enjoy the gorgeous scenery while camping on the Los Coyotes Reservation. On the Morongo Reservation, they visit the Malki Museum, where they get better acquainted with Cahuilla culture. The museum displays Cahuilla baskets, some of the best in

Playing games at the Junior Ranger Program, Agua Caliente

the world. There are lots of activities for tourists, but for the Cahuillas, the reservations are home.

There are many different businesses, including a recovery project. The Cabazon Reservation project helps take care of one of America's biggest pollution problems—spare tires. Instead of throwing all those tires in a landfill, making more garbage, the project recycles them into "crumb rubber," used for roads, fake turf, and dock bumpers. The Cahuillas are concerned that their land does not get more polluted; the project sets a good example for everyone.

The Cahuillas want to protect their beautiful canyons, filfera palm trees, deserts, and mountains for future generations. If they keep the land safe, they feel they'll be safe, too. That's why Cahuilla elders say, *mayemtiana kikitumay*, or "save the children."

Hiking through canyons, Agua Caliente

More facts about Cahuillas

Reservations/Communities: 10 reservations in southern California

Total population: 1,294 (1990 census)

Some people to learn about:
Rupert Costo [1906–1989], educator, newspaper publisher
Ruby Modesto [1913–1980], medicine woman
Katherine Siva Saubel [1920–], historian, museum educator

Neighbors: Chemehuevis, Luiseños, Mojaves, Quechans, Serranos

Performing Bird Songs at the Sherman Indian School, Riverside, California

Yurok (YUR-ik)

Drumming and singing in Klamath, California

Posing in a traditional Yurok outfit, complete with basket hat

The Yurok communities in northwestern California are near the Pacific Ocean, in redwood forests and on the Klamath River. In the Yurok language, they call themselves *Olekwo'l*, which means "persons."

If you are Yurok, you'd better like fish! Fish is one of their favorite foods, especially salmon and eels. Almost everybody goes to fish camp; sometimes kids stay up all night, listening to songs and old stories and helping the grown-ups process the catch. Before non-Indian commercial fishermen came to Yurok territory, there was enough salmon for everyone. Yurok ancestors made sure the salmon survived by leaving holes in the nets so some of the salmon could get through and go upstream to spawn. Today the Yuroks are leading the movement to protect traditional subsistence farming methods and natural resources like salmon.

Yurok basket makers use hazel, willow, spruce, and

Dancing together at a Yurok gathering

other woods in their beautiful and famous designs. The baskets are woven so tightly they can hold water. The California Indian Basketweavers Association educates people about the importance of protecting plants from extinction and the harmful effects of pesticides.

Did you know that basket hats are part of the Yuroks' native outfits? They are worn on special occasions like the Jump Dance Ceremony, part of Yurok religion. Every event has food, too. Acorn soup, a Yurok dish, is delicious and smooth as silk—but don't make it yourself. It's dangerous to eat poorly prepared acorns.

Since Yuroks live around so much water, they are really good boatbuilders. Yurok artist George Blake continues the redwood dugout canoe tradition. He uses many different tools to shape the huge log into a craft that dances on the rough river, able to withstand all the swirling and crashing water.

A long time ago Yurok children were taken far from home and put in government boarding schools. Today they attend schools with non-Native children, near their homes. Yurok leaders work hard at developing ways for adults to make a living so they don't have to leave their communities anymore. Harvesting salmon, raising flowers and vegetables in greenhouses, and operating campgrounds are all tribal industries employing Yuroks.

More facts about Yuroks

Reservations/Communities: one reservation and six rancherias in northern California

Total population: 4,444 (1990 census)

Some people to learn about:
Abby Abinanti [1947–], attorney
R. E. Bartow [1946–], artist
Susan Masten [1952–], tribal leader, political activist

Neighbors: Hupas, Karoks, Shastas, Tolowas, Klamaths

Swimming in the Klamath River

Lummi (LUM-ee)

Taking a big leap!

Faster and faster! Knowing the other canoes may catch up, the teams pull together as one and fly through the water! From May until August, the Lummis race their hand-carved canoes in the waters around their reservation. Their community is on an island and two peninsulas on the northwestern coast of Washington.

The Lummis have used the big war canoes for centuries; today teams compete with other Native peoples from all over. Carving the 50-foot canoes from huge cedar logs takes a lot of skill and patience, but Lummi artisans teach the craft.

School subjects center around learning Lummi traditions. People from other tribes come to learn about Lummi aquaculture at the tribe's Northwest Indian

Racing the longboat

Canoeing on Lummi Bay

College. Many parents work for the Lummis' large commercial fishing fleet and fish-processing plants. The Nation's modern salmon and shellfish hatchery is a place where fish are raised and studied to make sure there are enough to repopulate. Salmon is at the center of Lummi life, so the Lummis have a big ceremony when the salmon return to their waters to spawn.

Salmon travel all over, and sometimes the Lummi do, too! Youth dancers went to China on a cultural exchange in 2001. The children helped the Chinese people understand Lummi culture. Back at home, they celebrate Lummi *Stommish* (Water Festival) with canoe races, dances, arts and crafts, salmon barbecues, and ancient games like *Sla-hal*, a traditional gambling game.

The Lummis work hard to protect their land and fishing rights. Because of clear-cutting and illegal building on the reservation, there is erosion and damage to the waters and tidal lands. Protecting the natural resources is a main concern of the Lummis. They are replanting a conifer forest and trying other methods to stop the shore from eroding.

More facts about Lummis

Reservations/Communities: one reservation in Washington State

Total population: 3,125 (1990 census)

Some people to learn about:
Fran James [c. 1923–], basket weaver
Jewel James [1953–], master carver
Verne Johnson, Jr. [1952–1994], water rights activist

Neighbors: Noosacks, Sauk-Suiattles, Stillaguamishs, Swinomishs, Tulalips, Upper Skagits

Feasting on crab in Bellingham, Washington

Tsimshian (SIM-shee-an)

Looking for clams in Metlakatla

Celebrating a totem pole raising

The Tsimshians from Annette Island in southeastern Alaska live on the only Indian reservation in the state. Mountains, tidal pools, beaches, and lakes surround their town, Metlakatla. Do you think of snow when you think of Alaska? Tsimshians get a lot of rain, but it rarely gets very cold or very hot.

In the 1800s, a missionary convinced Tsimshian ancestors to move to Alaska from British Columbia. Living in the Pacific Ocean on an island is different from living in most places. There are no bridges connecting the Tsimshian nation to the mainland or other islands, so people travel by boat, ferry, and floatplanes. Some Tsimshians are ace pilots and own their aircraft.

Many Tsimshians are fishermen or work in related industries. If you visit, you can even buy salmon packaged in keepsake wooden boxes. The Annette Island

Packing Company is the only place in Alaska where you can tour a fish-processing plant.

During the summer, kids attend Culture Camp. Not only do they study the Tsimshian language, basketry, carving, blanket making, and beading, but they also go camping and swimming. And of course, they learn everything about fish, from catching it to cleaning it to smoking it!

Tsimshian kids are pretty good basketball players; they travel by ferry or floatplane to compete with other teams. Some young people travel with a dance troupe, too. The Git Lax Liksht'aa (People of the Island) Traditional Dancers have gone as far away as Hawaii to perform!

Totem-pole carving is an ancient art form. Totem poles tell a story. It's almost like reading a book. Master carver Jack Hudson teaches children paddle and mask carving as well as drawing.

Traditional potlatch ceremonies are celebrations of weddings, new totem poles, or the October salmon run. Tsimshian children look forward to the feasting, dancing, and gift giving. Tsimshian people also work to keep Annette Island beautiful. The hazardous debris left at an abandoned military base is being removed. Children help by doing litter patrol.

Getting the feel of carving a totem pole with Dad, David Boxley

More facts about Tsimshians

Reservations/Communities: one reservation on Annette Island, Alaska; villages in British Columbia, Canada

Total population: 2,157 (1990 census)

Some people to learn about:
David Boxley [1952–], wood sculptor
Janie Leask [1948–], political activist
Bert Ryan [1942–], metalsmith

Neighbors: Haidas, Kwakiutls, Tlingits in British Columbia, Canada

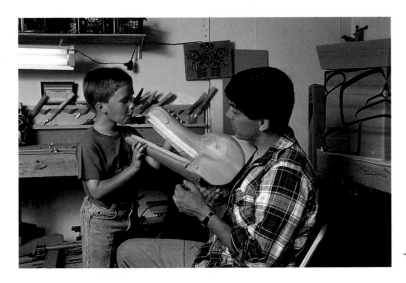
Talking with a transformation mask

Aleut (AL-ute)

Eating tasty wild celery on St. Paul Island

Making string figures on St. Paul Island

The Aleuts, or Unangan (oo-NUNG-an), as they call themselves, live on the Aleutian and Pribilof Islands in the westernmost part of Alaska. The treeless islands in the Aleutian chain stretch in a 1,200-mile arc where the Pacific Ocean meets the Bering Sea. The Pribilof Islands sit in the Bering Sea, north of the Aleutian Islands. Summers are short and winters are mild, but there is a lot of wind, fog, and unpredictable weather.

Since the Aleutian people live in the middle of the sea, they travel by boat and airplane more than by car. Sometimes the Pribilof Islands are called the Galapagos of the North, because there are so many different animals and birds there. Did you know that 70 percent of the world's fur seals come from here? They breed on the shores and near villages. Even though they may travel as far away as California or Japan, they always come back to have their babies. Many Aleuts feel a special bond with the marine mammals and try to take care of them.

On St. Paul Island there is a stewardship program where young people capture seals that have gotten tangled in ocean debris like fishing nets. The "noosers" remove the object that is wounding the animal and release it. The seals get mad, but after the debris is removed, they hump back into the sea and seem much happier. The kids feel happy, too, because they know they've saved the seals' lives!

Once in a while Aleuts hunt seal just for themselves, but they never waste anything. Elders teach children how to prepare the most delicious seal dishes.

In school, children study Unangan tunuu (oo-NUNG-an TOO-new), "our people's language." They also learn Aleut history. During World War II, the U.S. Army took over their islands and made most Aleuts leave for their safety. They were transported to southeast Alaska and had to live in run-down fish cannery buildings. There wasn't enough food and medicine, so many people died.

Searching for birds and reindeer as part of a stewardship program

After the war, the Aleuts returned to the islands. The U.S. government has not apologized to the Aleuts for treating them with such disrespect.

Many Aleut communities have wooden boardwalks and sandy beaches. Almost all have tall grasses that are woven into some of the most delicate baskets in the world. You can see them and other beautiful Unangam arts in many museums.

More facts about Aleuts

Reservations/Communities: 11 villages on the Aleutian and Pribilof Islands

Total population: 16,978

Some people to learn about:
John Hoover [1919–], wood sculptor
Jane Lind [contemporary], actor
Mary Youngblood [1950–], flautist

Neighbors: Yup'iks

Hopping ahead in the sack race at a 4th of July celebration

53

Yup'ik, Iñupiat
(YOU-pick)   (eh-NEW-pee-ot)

A successful catch at a Yup'ik fish camp in Kwethluk, Alaska

Ferrying provisions on an ice floe to Iñupiat spring hunting camp

The Yup'iks of southwest Alaska and the Iñupiats of north Alaska have very different languages, but they share some of the same customs. Most Yup'iks and Iñupiats have a subsistence way of life. That means they fish and hunt for survival, not for sport. Hunting for food is serious business; they always thank the animal for giving them food to eat.

The whole family shares in catching and preparing the salmon, as the catch has to last through the winter. Some parents work in the schools, government offices, radio and television stations, and sawmills. Still others earn a living by selling traditional arts of grass baskets, walrus ivory carvings, dolls, or the famous musk-ox wool clothing. Did you know that musk-ox wool is the lightest, warmest wool in the world?

You may think it snows all the time, but it doesn't. In the summer the tundra is covered with wildflowers, and children pick berries and wild celery. Kids attend summer camps like the Iñupiat Camp Sivunniigvik, which means "place of planning" in the Iñupiat language, to learn culture and language. It's fun learning traditional games like the blanket toss. Some say hunters could spot game over the horizon by bouncing so high.

In Yup'ik camps children learn many of the ancient dances that tell a story, along with some new ones, like "We Were Flying in a Plane and Almost Crashed!" There aren't many roads here, so people get around by plane or boat.

Flying high in the traditional
Iñupiat blanket toss game

Have you ever seen the World Eskimo-Indian Olympics on television? In July, Native people from all over compete in games like Ear Pull, Knuckle Hop, and Toe Kick. There's lots of dancing, singing, and feasting, too. Although it is competitive, children are usually taught to cooperate rather than compete. In the harsh northern environment, it is necessary to care for one another so everyone can survive.

More facts about Yup'iks and Iñupiats

Reservations/Communities: over 100 villages in north Alaska (Iñupiat) and southwest Alaska (Yup'ik); villages in Canada, Greenland, and Siberia

Total population: 54,761

Some people to learn about:
John Active [1948–], Yup'ik radio broadcaster, writer
Jeanie Greene [1952–], Iñupiat television host
Howard Rock [1911–1976], Iñupiat newspaper editor, artist

Neighbors: Aleuts, Athabascans

Camping out at Katmai National Park for the Yup'ik autumn seal trip

Hawaiian (hah-WHY-un)

Wading to shore in Honolulu

Studying a stream's ecosystem first hand, Honouliwai

Many people think of Hawaii as a place for vacations, with erupting volcanoes and hula dancing. For Hawaiians, it is home, where parents work and kids go to school. The Native Hawaiians live in a beautiful land in the middle of the Pacific Ocean, as their ancestors did for thousands of years.

Eight islands make up Hawaiian homeland. The people love the ocean, which surrounds them. The family is at the center of the communities, and sometimes everyone goes camping on the beach—children, parents, aunts, uncles, and grandparents.

Guess who taught the world to surf? Native Hawaiians. Since ancient times, they have practiced the sport. Today people come from all around the world to surf Hawaii's fantastic waves. One famous Hawaiian surfer, Duke Kahanamoku, was also an Olympic swimmer.

Do you know the Hawaiian language is still spoken? It is endangered, like many other Native languages. There are public school programs, however, where children can learn in both Hawaiian and English. On the island of Molokai, instructors like Kumi Puanani Johnston teach Hawaiian along with math, science, and reading. She takes her classes on field trips, like the one they took to *Hokule'a*.

Hokule'a is an outrigger canoe built in the same way as the Hawaiian ancestors built canoes. When *Hokule'a* visits the different islands, the crew helps children learn more about Hawaiian traditions. The people who built it wanted to prove that ancient Hawaiians navigated the seas without modern equipment like radar. Using the stars and other old ways to map

Weeding before planting a new crop of kalo, Honouliwai

A recess time plunge at Mo'omomi Beach on Moloka'i

More facts about Hawaiians

Reservations/Communities: communities on eight islands

Total population: 401,162

Some people to learn about:
Alani Apio [1965–], actor, dramatist
Pualani Kanaka'ole Kanahele
    [contemporary], educator
Haunani-Kay Trask [contemporary],
    university professor, political activist

Neighbors: Samoans, Tahitians, Tongans

routes, *Hokule'a* has sailed to New Zealand, Tahiti, and Easter Island.

There are three active volcanoes on the island of Hawaii: Kilauea, Mauna Loa, and Loihi. Kilauea is one of the most active volcanoes on Earth. It has been called the "drive up" volcano because it is easy to get near many of its active areas.

Although Hawaii is a beautiful place to live, it is getting polluted. Native Hawaiians are concerned about that and have organizations helping to protect nearly 1,000 plants and animals in danger of extinction. There are also groups working to regain land rights.

Hugging at Kamehameha Day, Honolulu

57

Urban People

Performing a hoop dance at the Museum of Man, San Diego, California

Playing in the park, Chicago, Illinois

Non-Native people are sometimes surprised to see Indian people in the subway or on a bus when they're wearing traditional jewelry or clothing. That is because they don't know that over half of all American Indians live in cities. Of course, Indian people generally wear regalia for special occasions; most times, they dress like other people in cities. It is a stereotype when people expect Indian people to dress the same way and live in the same place as they did in the past.

Most large cities have Indian centers, and some have special Indian schools, like the Heart of the Earth School in Minneapolis. Most centers attract people from many different Indian tribes, but other centers near reservations are more representative of a particular Indian nation. The centers provide a place where urban Native people can get help with legal issues, housing, health concerns, and employment. They are also a place to socialize with other Indian people and attend cultural events like powwows, plays, and feasts.

The American Indian Community House in New York City has an art gallery and a performing arts department. New York is famous for its art, music, and theater; many American Indian artists want to be part of the New York art world, too. New York also has special programs, like Nitchen, Inc., to help Indian people strengthen and support each other and their families. Since urban Indian people live in communities with all

Leaving the subway station, New York, New York

Hanging out on the steps of the National Museum of the American Indian, New York, New York

kinds of Americans, these organizations help them preserve their own cultures.

Most families came to the cities to find employment. In the 20th century, the U.S. government forced many Indian people off the reservations and into the cities. Many children go back to their original communities on weekends and summer vacations, but some have considered the cities home for generations. Non-Indians in urban areas have the opportunity to attend festivals and visit Indian centers and museums to meet Indian people and learn about Native cultures.

Swinging over the skyline, St. Paul, Minnesota

The ten cities with the largest Native American populations:

New York, NY	87,241
Los Angeles, CA	53,092
Phoenix, AZ	35,093
Tulsa, OK	30,227
Oklahoma City, OK	29,001
Anchorage, AK	26,995
Albuquerque, NM	22,047
Chicago, IL	20,898
San Diego, CA	16,178
Houston, TX	15,743

Some people to learn about:

John E. Echohawk, Pawnee [1945–], director of Native American Rights Fund, Denver, CO

W. Richard West, Southern Cheyenne [1943–], director of the National Museum of the American Indian, Washington, DC

Rosemary Richmond, Mohawk [1937–], director of American Indian Community House, New York, NY

Resources for Further Study

Here are some nonfiction titles about nations described in this book, as well as a few books with poems about Native American life today.

Books for Children

Begay, Shonto. *Navajo: Visions and Voices Across the Mesa*. New York: Scholastic, 1995.

Champagne, Duane. *Native America: Portrait of the Peoples*. Detroit: Visible Ink Press, 1994.

Crum, Robert. *Eagle Drum: On the Powwow Trail with a Young Grass Dancer*. New York: Four Winds Press, 1994.

Griffin-Pierce, Trudy. *The Encyclopedia of Native America*. New York: Viking Press, 1995.

Hawaiian Word Book. Illustrated by Robin Yoko Burningham. Honolulu, HI: Bess Press, 1983.

Hazen-Hammond, Susan. *Thunder Bear and Ko: The Buffalo Nation and Nambe Pueblo*. New York: Dutton Children's Books, 1999.

Hirschfelder, Arlene B. and Beverly R. Singer, eds. *Rising Voices: Writings of Young Native Americans*. New York: Scribner's, 1992.

Hoyt-Goldsmith, Diane. *Arctic Hunter* [Iñupiat]. New York: Holiday House, 1992.

Hoyt-Goldsmith, Diane. *Buffalo Days* [Crow]. New York: Holiday House, 1997.

Hoyt-Goldsmith, Diane. *Cherokee Summer*. New York: Holiday House, 1993.

Hoyt-Goldsmith, Diane. *Lacrosse: The National Game of the Iroquois*. New York: Holiday House, 1998.

Hoyt-Goldsmith, Diane. *Potlatch: A Tsimshian Celebration*. New York: Holiday House, 1997.

Keegan, Marcia. *Pueblo Boy: Growing Up in Two Worlds*. New York: Cobblehill Books, 1991.

Keegan, Marcia. *Pueblo Girls: Growing Up in Two Worlds*. Santa Fe: Clear Light Publishers, 1999.

Krull, Kathleen. *One Nation, Many Tribes: How Kids Live in Milwaukee's Indian Community*. New York: Lodestar Books, 1995.

Left Hand Bull, Jacqueline and Suzanne Haldane. *Lakota Hoop Dancer*. New York: Dutton Children's Books, 1999.

McMillan, Bruce. *Salmon Summer* [Aleut]. Boston: Houghton Mifflin, 1998.

National Museum of the American Indian, Smithsonian Institution. *When the Rain Sings: Poems by Young Native Americans*. New York: Simon & Schuster Books for Young Readers, 1999.

Peters, Russell M. *Clambake: A Wampanoag Tradition*. Minneapolis: Lerner Publications, 1992.

Regguinti, Gordon. *The Sacred Harvest: Ojibway Wild Rice Gathering*. Minneapolis: Lerner Publications, 1992.

Roessel, Monty. *Songs from the Loom: A Navajo Girl Learns to Weave*. Minneapolis: Lerner Publications, 1995.

Waldman, Carl. *Encyclopedia of Native American Tribes*, rev. ed. New York: Facts on File, 1999.

Wittstock, Laura W. *Ininatig's Gift of Sugar: Traditional Native Sugarmaking* [Ojibway]. Minneapolis: Lerner Publications, 1993.

Books for Parents and Educators

Hirschfelder, Arlene and Yvonne Beamer. *Native Americans Today: Resources and Activities for Educators, Grades 4-8*. Englewood, CO: Teacher Ideas Press, 2000.

Hirschfelder, Arlene, Paulette Fairbanks Molin, and Yvonne Wakim. *American Indian Stereotypes in the World of Children: A Reader and Bibliography*, 2nd ed. Lanham, MD: Scarecrow Press, 1999.

Johansen, Bruce E. and Donald A. Grinde, Jr. *The Encyclopedia of Native American Biography: Six Hundred Life Stories of Important People from Powhatan to Wilma Mankiller.* New York: Henry Holt and Co., 1997.

Malinowski, Sharon, ed. *The Gale Encyclopedia of Native American Tribes.* 4 vols. Detroit: Gale, 1998.

Riley, Patricia, ed. *Growing Up Native American: An Anthology.* New York: Avon, 1993.

Slapin, Beverly and Doris Seale. *Through Indian Eyes: The Native Experience in Books for Children.* Los Angeles: American Indian Studies Center, University of California, 1998.

Magazines and Newspapers for Children

Canku Ota (Many Paths): *A Newsletter Celebrating Native America.* http://www.turtletrack.org

Faces, the Magazine About People. Articles about Indian cultures.

Indian Country Today. Weekly newspaper covers national issues. http://www.indiancountry.com

Native Peoples: Arts & Lifeways. Quarterly magazine dedicated to the sensitive portrayal of Native peoples of the Americas. http://www.nativepeoples.com

News from Indian Country. Newspaper published twice a month. http://www.indiancountrynews.com

Organizations

American Indian Science and Engineering Society
2305 Revard SE, Suite 200, Albuquerque, NM 87106
(505) 765-1052
http://www.aises.org

Bureau of Indian Affairs
1849 C Street NW, Washington, DC 20245
(202) 208-3711

Council for Indian Education
1240 Burlington Ave., Billings, MT 59102-4224
(406) 248-3465
http://www.cie-mt.org

Cradleboard Teaching Project
1191 Kuhio Highway, Kapaa, HI 96746
(808) 822-3111
http://www.cradleboard.org

Oyate
2702 Mathews Street, Berkeley, CA 94702
(510) 848-6700
http://www.oyate.org

Web Sites

Alaska Native Heritage Center
http://www.alaskanative.net

Center for Oral History, University of Hawaii at Manoa
http://www2.soc.hawaii.edu/css/oral_hist/

Flags of Native People of the United States
http://hometown.aol.com/Donh523/navapage/index.htm

Hanksville (homepages of Native authors)
http://www.hanksville.org

Hawaii Nation Homepage
http:// www.hawaii-nation.org

National Museum of the American Indian
http://www.nmai.si.edu

Native American Sites (provides access to K-12 sites)
http://www.nativeculture.com/lisamitten/indians.html

Native American Sports Council
http://www.nascsports.org

Native Nations (official and unofficial tribal sites)
http://www.kstrom.net/isk/tribes/tribes.htm

Native Web (culture from the Arctic to Tierra del Fuego)
http://www.nativeweb.org

Glossary

aquaculture – farming, processing, breeding, and raising fish or other water species

confederacy – a political union of several nations formed for mutual support or common action

hominy (*holhponi*) – corn processed in a special way

kalo – a plant that Native Hawaiian people believe to have the greatest life force of all foods. It is also known as taro, and is used to make a food called poi.

nation – a group of people who share a common history, culture, homeland, government, and often, language.

outrigger – a large canoe equipped with supports so that it will not be easily overturned

powwow – a festival where Indian people and guests enjoy dancing, singing, music, and food

quahog – a thick-shelled edible clam

rancheria – a land reserved for Indian people in California, similar to a reservation

regalia – culturally-inspired clothing, headdresses, and other decorations worn by Native people during their ceremonies or powwows

reservation – a piece of land that belongs to and is used by one or more groups of American Indians. Reservations are not public property, and they are not part of the states surrounding them.

sovereignty – independence as a nation, state, city, or government. Native American governments are separate from the United States, and can make and enforce their own laws.

stereotype – to characterize an entire group and all of its members in specific ways, usually negatively

subsistence farming – a type of farming in which crops are produced for farmers and their family members, not for cash sales

syllabary – a system of writing in which each sound of a spoken language is expressed by a different character or letter

tipi – a cone-shaped house made out of wooden poles and buffalo hides. Long ago, the tipi was a movable dwelling, ideal for Native peoples who followed buffalo herds.

totem pole – a tall pole cut from a single log, carved and painted with a series of figures and symbols with special tribal meanings. A pole can honor an individual or tell a traditional story.

treaty – a formal agreement between nations

tribe – a group of people having a common cultural ancestry who speak the same language, share a history that stretches far back in time, and have the same traditions and values. A tribe is also a political group living under a leader or chief. Nations are often called tribes by some non-Indians.

wampum – white tubular beads made from Atlantic whelks and purple rectangular beads made from quahog shells. They were rolled smooth on sandstone, then used to record agreements.

wickiup – a cone-shaped or domed dwelling with a pole frame covered with brush, grass, or reeds

wild rice (*manoomin*) – a grass with an edible grain that grows along the western Great Lakes

Acknowledgments

A MESSAGE FROM MAYA AJMERA, THE EXECUTIVE DIRECTOR OF THE GLOBAL FUND FOR CHILDREN:

Children of Native America Today grew out of a wonderfully fulfilling collaboration between Shakti for Children and the book's distinguished co-authors, Arlene Hirschfelder and Yvonne Wakim Dennis. We are proud and delighted to include *Children of Native America Today* in our growing collection of multicultural books. Evoking the Hindi word for empowerment, Shakti for Children books are designed to teach children to value diversity and to grow into productive, caring citizens of the world. Shakti for Children is a program of the Global Fund for Children, a nonprofit organization committed to advancing the human rights of young people around the world.

Arlene Hirschfelder first approached me three years ago about developing a book on Native American children in the United States. I was immediately excited about the idea of portraying Native American children through positive and empowering images and by the opportunity to inform young people about the vast diversity and heritage of Native American culture. A year later, I asked Arlene to develop a book similar to our first Shakti for Children title, *Children from Australia to Zimbabwe*. With major support from the Bank of America Foundation and additional support from the Flora Family Foundation and the W. K. Kellogg Foundation, *Children of Native America Today* was born. Arlene teamed up with Yvonne Wakim Dennis, another well-respected writer of Native American history, to co-author the book. I honor Arlene and Yvonne's sensitive and strong voice for Native American children everywhere.

The photographs in this book portray the beauty and strength of Native children in the United States. The photographers are owed deep gratitude for aligning themselves with this project and with the mission of the Global Fund for Children. Without their commitment and photographs, there would be no book.

Deepest thanks to Joan Shifrin of the Global Fund for Children for her creative insights. I also wish to thank the following individuals who have provided guidance and support for this book: Caroline Boitano, Donna Chavis, Lynn Drury, Paul Fulton, Mary Hewlett, Kayron Maynor, Marvin McKinney, Buffy Sainte-Marie, Susan Sherman, Kelly Swanson Turner, John H.T. Wilson, Rick West, and the Board of Directors of the Global Fund for Children.

I am gratified that a portion of the proceeds from sales of *Children of Native America Today* will be donated to community-based programs serving Native American children in the United States. This in the end speaks volumes about our commitment to all children.

A MESSAGE FROM THE AUTHORS:

Maya Ajmera's vision for humanity has inspired us and countless others. Our deepest gratitude to all the photographers whose creativity and generosity make this book possible. Special thanks to Buffy Sainte-Marie and Dagmar Thorpe, who are wonderful examples for all the children of America. Special thanks to Bill and Barbara Ascher, who were the networkers for this book.

Our heartfelt thanks to the following people who helped beyond measure: Nadema Agard, Matthew Anderson and Chris Goodenow, Derrill Bazzy, Freddie Bell, Cheryl Walsh Bellville, Tony Belcastro, Carol Bruchac, Gwendolyn Cates, Raquel Chapa, Kathleen Doherty, Christy Fletcher, Steve Gambaro, John Goodwin, Kay Humphrey, Adriana Ignacio, Kimberly Puanani Johnston, Ceely King, Taina Landron, Louise Lampman Larivee, Robert Lyttle and Carletta Tilousi, Paulette F. Molin, Kalani Mondoy, Rosalind Morgan, Delphine Nelson, Christopher Sepulveda, Beverly R. Singer, Justine Smith, Berta Welch, Marilyn "Angel" Wynn, Diana Yolinemi, and Ray Young Bear.

Yvonne Wakim Dennis is ever grateful to all her healers: Nancy Fischman Rubin, Radha Baum, Fredlina Munroe, Rosie Nerl, David Winston; Dr. Zinaida Pelkey, Dr. Lee Piper, Dr. Susan Levine, and Dr. Steven Lowy. She and Arlene thank all their friends, relatives, and children of Native America, and ask forgiveness for any mistakes.

Index and Photographers' Credits